ENIGMAS *of* HISTORY

THE MYSTERIES OF EGYPT'S PYRAMIDS

WITHDRAWN

WORLD
BOOK

a Scott Fetzer company
Chicago
www.worldbook.com

World Book edition of "Enigmas de la historia" by Editorial Sol 90.

Enigmas de la historia
Las pirámides de Egipto

This edition licensed from Editorial Sol 90 S.L.
Copyright 2013 Editorial Sol S.L. All rights reserved.

English-language revised edition copyright 2015
World Book, Inc.
Enigmas of History
The Mysteries of Egypt's Pyramids

World Book, Inc.
233 North Michigan Avenue, Suite 2000
Chicago, Illinois 60601 U.S.A.

For information about other World Book publications,
visit our website at **www.worldbook.com** or call
1-800-967-5325.

Library of Congress Cataloging-in-Publication Data

Pirámides de Egipto. English
 The mysteries of Egypt's pyramids. -- English-language
revised edition.
    pages cm. -- (Enigmas of history)
  Includes index.
  Summary: "An exploration of the questions and mysteries surrounding the pyramids of Egypt. Features
include a map, fact boxes, biographies of famous experts
on ancient Egypt, places to see and visit, a glossary,
further readings, and index"-- Provided by publisher.
  ISBN 978-0-7166-2677-0
  1. Pyramids--Egypt--Juvenile literature. I. World
Book, Inc. II. Title.
 DT63.P5713 2015
 932--dc23
                                2015013429
Enigmas of History Set ISBN: 978-0-7166-2670-1

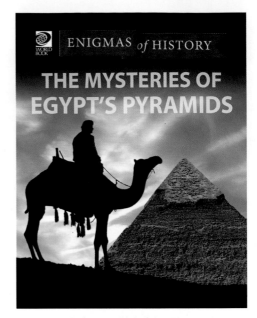

The pyramid of Pharaoh Khafre at Giza.

© naglestock.com/Alamy

Printed in China by Shenzhen Donnelley
Printing Co., Ltd., Guangdong Province
1st printing May 2015

Staff

Contents

A Genuine Marvel of Building Skill

The magnificent pyramids of Egypt were built for great pharaohs (*FAIR ohz*), what the ancient Egyptians called their kings. The largest, called the Great Pyramid, is the oldest of the seven ancient wonders of the world and the only wonder that remains today. The step pyramid of Zoser (pronounced *zoh zuhr* and sometimes spelled Djoser)—which was the work of the master builder Imhotep (*ihm HOH tehp*)—was the first of these enormous stone monuments to be built. This pyramid was built in Saqqarah (*suh KAHR uh*), an ancient burial ground near present-day Cairo. Zoser's pyramid came before a golden age of advancement in science and technical progress that characterized ancient Egypt's Old Kingdom (about 2650-2150 B.C.)—the time of the pyramids. The most impressive of these massive structures, the three pyramids at Giza, were built to memorialize members of a single Egyptian *dynasty* (royal family): Snefru

(*SNEF roo*), who ruled from about 2597 to 2547 B.C.; his son Khufu (*KOO foo*), who was called Cheops by the Greeks; and grandson Khafre (*KAHF rey*). Under the reign of these pharaohs, million of tons of stone were carved out of quarries, moved, and hoisted into place to build these masterpieces of architecture and engineering using nothing more than simple wooden and copper tools and immense amounts of human labor.

The Pyramid of Khafre marked the end of an era of construction of the most enormous pyramids. The one built for his son, Menkaure (*men kahr*), would begin a new era of smaller, more modest, pyramids for pharaohs. By the time of the Middle Kingdom (about 1975-1640 B.C.) and New Kingdom (about 1539-1075 B.C.), the pyramids were already seen as relics of a glorious, bygone time in the history of ancient Egypt.

History has remained mostly silent about how the pyramids were built. This has allowed *Egyptologists* (scholars who study ancient Egypt) to propose many theories about their construction—some more likely than others. Most theories fall into two branches. One branch is rooted in descriptions of the ancient Greek historian Herodotus (*hih ROD uh tuhs–* 484?-425? B.C.). Herodotus visited Giza some 2,000 years after the pyramids were finished. He claimed the massive stone blocks were lifted one on top of the other by thousands of slaves. Another branch of thought is that the Egyptians used a series of ramps, either a straight front ramp or a zig-zag ramp going up the sides, to slide the massive stone blocks into place to construct the pyramids.

Some Egyptologists also consider a different idea—that the pyramids were built from the inside out. Some engineers think that the huge stone blocks could have been delivered through a short ramp on the outside of the construction. Later, blocks would have been placed by means of an inner ramp, covered by a *vault* (arched ceiling) built within the monument at the beginning of construction. Once the pyramid was far enough along, the worker could bring blocks from outside through the inner ramp to build the remaining top portion of the pyramid.

The ancient Egyptians made many other outstanding contributions to the development of civilization beginning almost 5,000 years ago. Their way of life thrived for over 2,000 years and so became one of the longest lasting civilizations in history. The ancient Egyptians created the world's first national government, basic forms of arithmetic, and a 365-day calendar. They invented a form of picture writing called hieroglyphics (*HY uhr uh GLIHF ihks*). They also invented *papyrus* (puh PY ruhs), a paperlike writing material made from fibers from the stems of papyrus, a reedlike water plant common in the Nile River. The Egyptian religion emphasized life after death, a belief that was central to the building of the pyramids. And, they built great cities in which many skilled architects, doctors, engineers, painters, and sculptors worked. The best-known achievements of the ancient Egyptians, however, are the pyramids they built.

An Arab proverb from around A.D. 1100 claims *Man fears time, but time fears the pyramids*. Read along as we explore the pyramids of ancient Egypt—timeless marvels of architectural and engineering skill—which serve as the most spectacular reminders of the glory of this ancient people. And find out about the many mysteries surrounding the pyramids that remain to be solved.

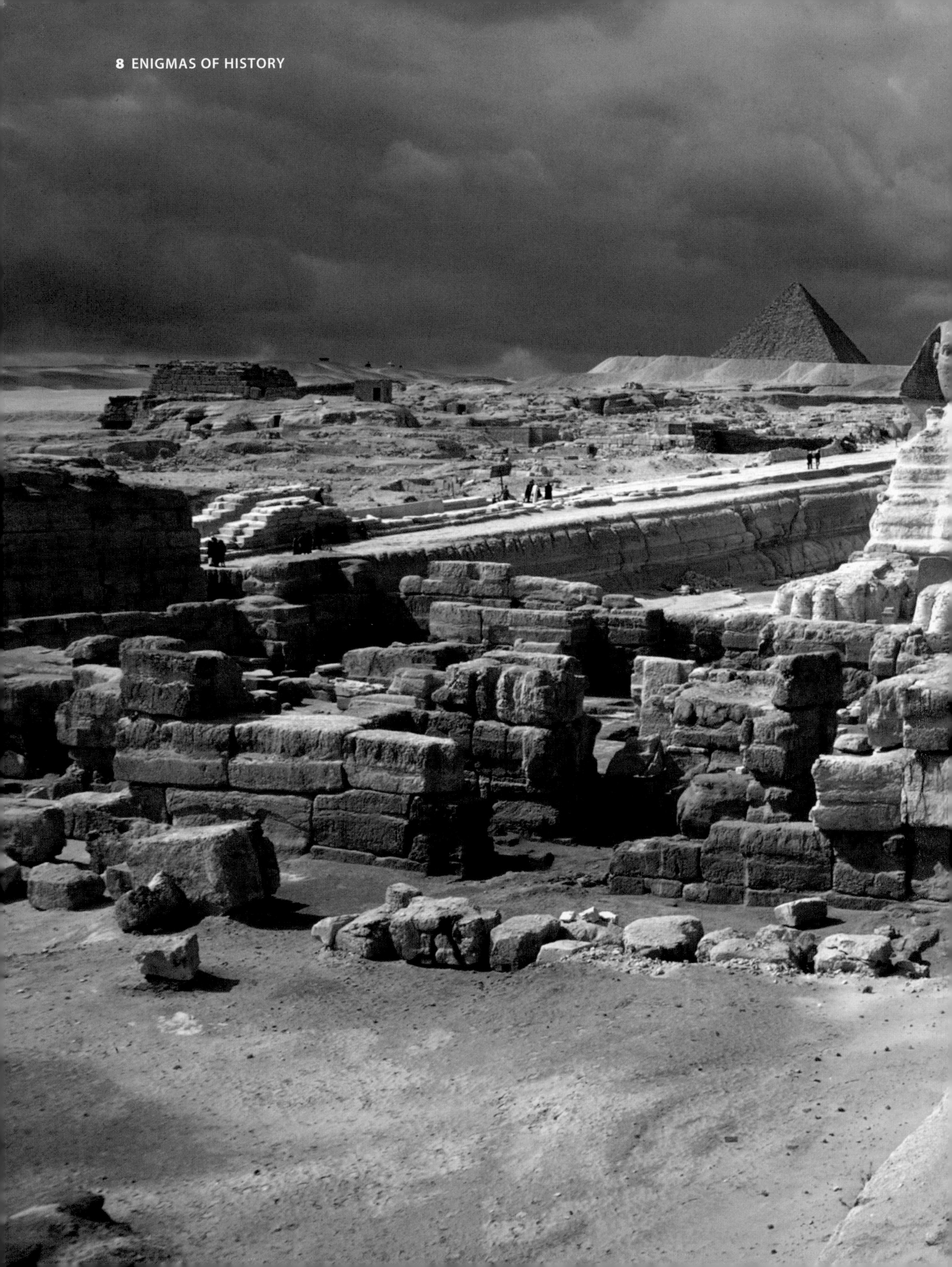

THE JEWELS OF GIZA
In the Egyptian city of Giza, the pyramids of the pharaohs Khafre (right) and Menkaure (left) rise behind the Great Sphinx. The sphinx is an imaginary creature of ancient myth. According to various stories, the sphinx had the body of a lion and the head of a human, falcon, or ram.

Important Pyramids

They are the most important architectural creation of ancient Egypt. A fundamental part of the pyramids was devoted to the worship of the *pharaohs*, the kings of ancient Egypt. Their primary purpose was to serve as burial monuments, but many pyramids were never actually used as tombs.

The plain of Giza

Although Egypt has at least 120 pyramids, those at Giza are the most famous.

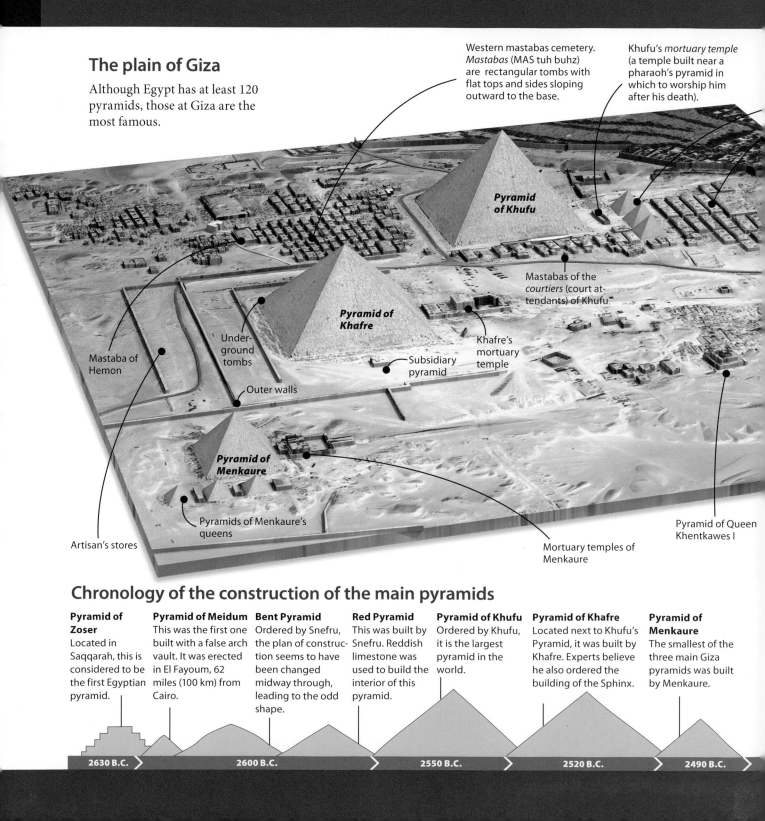

Western mastabas cemetery. *Mastabas* (MAS tuh buhz) are rectangular tombs with flat tops and sides sloping outward to the base.

Khufu's *mortuary temple* (a temple built near a pharaoh's pyramid in which to worship him after his death).

Pyramid of Khufu

Mastabas of the *courtiers* (court attendants) of Khufu

Mastaba of Hemon

Underground tombs

Pyramid of Khafre

Khafre's mortuary temple

Subsidiary pyramid

Outer walls

Pyramid of Menkaure

Artisan's stores

Pyramids of Menkaure's queens

Mortuary temples of Menkaure

Pyramid of Queen Khentkawes I

Chronology of the construction of the main pyramids

Pyramid of Zoser
Located in Saqqarah, this is considered to be the first Egyptian pyramid.

Pyramid of Meidum
This was the first one built with a false arch vault. It was erected in El Fayoum, 62 miles (100 km) from Cairo.

Bent Pyramid
Ordered by Snefru, the plan of construction seems to have been changed midway through, leading to the odd shape.

Red Pyramid
This was built by Snefru. Reddish limestone was used to build the interior of this pyramid.

Pyramid of Khufu
Ordered by Khufu, it is the largest pyramid in the world.

Pyramid of Khafre
Located next to Khufu's Pyramid, it was built by Khafre. Experts believe he also ordered the building of the Sphinx.

Pyramid of Menkaure
The smallest of the three main Giza pyramids was built by Menkaure.

2630 B.C.   2600 B.C.   2550 B.C.   2520 B.C.   2490 B.C.

How Long Did It Take to Build a Pyramid?

Experts believe that the architect who directed the construction at Giza spent almost two years planning the work. There was a schedule set for the tasks, according to the seasons, and for each activity as permitted by religion. According to this plan, the first 1,000 days were spent placing the first line of stones. The next 1,000 days were spent in finishing the king's chamber inside the pyramid, and 1,000 days later the pyramid was finished.

Map of the Egyptian pyramids

The Egyptian pyramids are located on the west bank of the Nile River and near villages, perhaps to provide the labor force needed for construction.

Tombs of Queen Hetepheres I

Great Sphinx

Temple of the Sphinx

Valley temple of Khafre

Abu Rawash

Magnified area

Giza

Cairo

Zawyet el-Aryan

Abusir

Dahshur

Saqqarah

Lisht

Mazghuna

Seila

Meidum

LOWER EGYPT

Hawara

Illahun

Eastern Desert

Pyramid of Pepi II
Erected at Saqqarah, the inside rooms contained writings that provide information about ancient Egyptian religion.

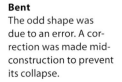

2250 B.C.

Types of pyramids

The Egyptian pyramids can be classified into three types according to their shape:

Bent
The odd shape was due to an error. A correction was made mid-construction to prevent its collapse.

Smooth
On a square base, it becomes progressively smaller towards the top.

Step
Consists of six *truncated* (cut off) pyramids on a rectangular base, narrowing towards the tip.

The Pyramids, Symbols of Eternal Life

More than 4,500 years after their construction, the pyramids of Egypt continue to fire our imagination. How were they built? What exactly was their purpose?

A sacred river splits the land into two. It runs from south to north and ends in the sea, blossoming out like a lotus flower. The land of the living is found on its east bank, where the sun God Ra (also spelled Re) comes into the world each day. On the west bank, where after the passing of each day the Sun is swallowed by Nut, Goddess of the Sky, lies the land of the dead, the resting place of the departed. The ancient Egyptians believed the course of the sun was Ra's ship crossing the ocean of the sky. Ra was renewed during the night to be reborn in the early hours of the morning. From the earliest days of their civilization, the ancient Egyptians believed their *pharaohs* (kings) were gods. To the ancient Egyptians, the pharaoh was the living person of the god Horus on Earth. And, like a god, the pharaoh had a more noble destiny than other mortals: after his life on Earth, he was fated to a heavenly existence. The pharaoh had a place on the ship of the sun and made the daily journey across the sky at the side of Ra.

Although *Egyptologists* (scholars who study ancient Egypt) know quite a bit about the origins of Egyptian civilization, they do not all agree when it comes to defining the different ages and periods of its history. Different timeframes are given with differences that range from 50 to 200 years. However, much is known about the details of daily Egyptian life, as well as of their social organization, customs, and beliefs during the Old Kingdom (about 2650-2150 B.C.) from painted murals and texts discovered by researchers.

It was during the Old Kingdom that the most magnificent pyramids were built. It was during the Old Kingdom that the Great Pyramid of Giza was erected as the tomb of pharaoh Khufu. It is the largest of the pyramids in Egypt. It was also during this era that the Osiris myth, closely connected with the development of Egyptian funeral rites, and so also with the pyramids, might have taken shape. The god Osiris represented royalty and was the central figure in Egypt's most popular myth. In Egyptian belief, during his reign the pharaoh held the dignity of the god Horus. After the pharaoh died, he would become Osiris, who had triumphed over death.

Egyptologists are not sure whether the pyramids were meant to be royal tombs or whether they merely served as a resting place for the *ka* (spirit) of the pharaoh. There is no doubt that the pyramids were part of the complex variety of religious ceremonies surrounding the pharaohs and their journey to the afterlife. But that sort of certainty is rare amid the many

PYRAMID OF KHAFRE
This pyramid preserves some of the limestone casing stones that covered the outer face of the structure. These stones gave the pyramid a smooth appearance.

questions that still surround the pyramids. The unanswered questions challenge science and provide a fertile field for many fantastic speculations about the pyramids. The remains of at least 120 Egyptian pyramids can be seen today, all located on the western side of the Nile River valley, in the land of the dead. They were built during the earliest period of Egyptian civilization that spanned more than 2,000 years.

Imhotep, a great architect and statesman, built the first known pyramid for the pharaoh Zoser in about 2650 B.C. Zoser's tomb rose in a series of giant steps and is called the Step Pyramid. This pyramid still stands at the site of the ancient Egyptian city of Memphis, near Cairo.

The first smooth-sided pyramid was built about 2600 B.C. It still stands at Meidum, 62 miles (100

kilometers) south of Cairo. It began as a stepped pyramid, but the steps were filled in with stones to give the pyramid smooth, sloping sides.

The pyramids of Giza stand on the west bank of the Nile River outside Cairo. There are 10 pyramids at Giza, including three of the largest and best preserved of all Egyptian pyramids. These three pyramids, built for the Old Kingdom pharaohs Khufu, Khafre, and Menkaure, have come to symbolize all of ancient Egypt. A huge statue, called the Great Sphinx, with the body of a lion and head of a man, was probably built for Khafre. It stands near his pyramid. These monuments are a continuing subject of fascination as the creations of an ancient culture that was as sophisticated as it is puzzling. Most notable is the Great Pyramid, first and largest of the Giza pyramids. The Pharaoh

Khufu ordered his architect to design and build this wonder of the ancient world around 2580 B.C. It contains more than 2 million stone blocks that average 2.5 tons (2.3 metric tons) each. The pyramid was originally 481 feet (147 meters) tall, but some of its upper stones are gone now, and it stands about 450 feet (140 meters) high. Its base covers about 13 acres (5 hectares).

The Egyptians built massive stone pyramids only during a single 500-year period: The Old Kingdom. Thieves broke into nearly all of these pyramids, stole the gold and treasures they contained, and sometimes destroyed the bodies of the pharaohs. In the period called the Middle Kingdom that followed (approximately 1975-1640 B.C.), pyramids decreased in size and were of a lower quality. During the Middle Kingdom, pyra-

NECROPOLIS

The pyramids of Giza and the Great Sphinx (top left) are the most visible monuments of a *necropolis* (city of the dead) that also included other cemeteries, as well as homes and workshops for the workers who built them.

HIEROGLYPHICS

The writing system of the ancient Egyptians (top right) was based on a system of pictures that represented sounds and words. After several years of research, the French scholar Jean-François Champollion was able to decipher Egyptian hieroglyphs in 1822.

mids were built at Hawara, Illahun, Lisht, and Dahshur—near what is now Cairo. The remains of these smaller pyramids are still impressive.

Later Egyptian kings stopped using pyramids and built secret tombs in cliffs. In the New Kingdom (about 1539–1075 B.C.), pyramids only appear as external elements of some of these royal tombs. However, rulers of the kingdom of Kush, south of Egypt in Nubia (now in Sudan), built pyramids after the end of the New Kingdom, long after they were no longer used in Egypt.

ADMIRED BY GREECE AND ROME

The ancient Greek scholar Aristotle referred to the pyramids during the 300's B.C., in his work *Politics*. He pointed out that they would have served to keep the population busy and prevent plots against the phara-

ohs. The Greek historian Herodotus gives a detailed description of the pyramids and the method used to construct them. He attributed the work to slaves using pulleys and other simple machines to move the huge stone blocks into position. Some historians think that Herodotus may not have actually traveled to Egypt and only based his writings on the many stories and legends that circulated during his time in around 450 B.C. The Giza Pyramids were already 2,000 years old at that time.

The Romans also had a great fascination with Egypt and the pyramids. The Romans conquered Egypt and incorporated a number of Egyptian myths and gods into their culture. Roman nobles also began using small pyramids to mark their own graves during the first centuries A.D. As Egypt was incorporated into the

Roman empire, some Roman emperors even came to consider themselves as pharaohs. The importation of many Egyptian goods contributed to the popularity of Egyptian styles among the wealthy citizens of Rome. The Romans also imported Egyptian scientific knowledge about medicine, mathematics, and astronomy.

The Middle Ages was from about the 400's to the 1400's, and for most of that time people were unsure about how and why the pyramids were built. It wasn't until the Renaissance in the late 1300's that European scholars thought about the construction and possible purpose of the pyramids. At this time, legends had spread about spirits that inhabited them and fantastic treasures hidden inside. In the Arab world of that time, there were rumors of strange rooms hidden in the depths of the pyramids, as well as other mysterious secrets they held.

By the early the 1800's, as increased travel and communication between Europe and the Middle East developed, Egypt became important in conflicts between European powers. The expedition by French emperor Napoleon I in 1798 was perhaps the most important event in the development of the scientific study of ancient Egypt, called *Egyptology*.

Napoleon arrived in Alexandria, Egypt, on July 2, with 300 ships and more than 50,000 men, including 154 scientists. His aim was to disrupt Great Britain's trade routes to their colony of India. Twenty days later, Napoleon defeated the *Mamluks*, Egypt's military rulers, in the Battle of the Pyramids near Cairo. On August 22, he founded the Institute of Egypt. By September, French scientists were already working at the pyramids in Giza. Among them was scientist Dominique Vivant Denon, author of *Travels in Lower and Upper Egypt* (1802), in which he described

his journey down the Nile in 1799. Denon described the ruins at the ancient Egyptian cities of Thebes, Karnak, Luxor, and Aswan. Many scholars believe the publication of his book marks the official birth of Egyptology.

In 1799, during Napoleon's campaigns in Egypt, a French officer in the engineering corps discovered a large piece of black granite covered with Greek and Egyptian writing, half buried in the mud outside of Rosetta, a city near Alexandria. The language and writing of ancient Egypt had been a puzzle for scholars for hundreds of years. Finally Jean-François Champollion, a French historian and *linguist* (expert on languages) used the Rosetta Stone to solve the puzzle. Using the Greek writing on the stone as a guide, he studied the proper names in the Greek text and was able to pick out the same names in the Egyptian writing. This enabled him to learn the meaning of many of the Egyptian characters. In 1822, Champollion published a pamphlet containing the results of his work. This pamphlet at last enabled scholars to read the literature of ancient Egypt.

Napoleon had the writings of the many scholars who worked in Egypt published in a multivolume series called *Description of Egypt*, from 1809 to 1829. At this time scholars understood that the pyramids had a single function: as burial sites for pharaohs, who ruled ancient Egypt with absolute power. This idea continued throughout much of the 1900's. Today Egyptologists know that the function of the pyramids in the Old Kingdom of ancient Egypt was somewhat more complex.

THE LEADING RESEARCHERS

Among the notable scholars who studied the history of ancient Egypt and the pyramids, one of the earliest

Zahi Hawass
(1947-)

In 2002, Hawass served as Secretary General of the Supreme Council of Antiquities of Egypt, a post he left in late 2009 when he was appointed Deputy Minister of Culture. He left the office in 2011. Among his greatest achievements are the identification of the *mummy* (preserved body) of Hatshepsut and the discovery of new passages in the Great Pyramid.

DEDICATION Hawass has worked to bring the treasures of ancient Egypt at foreign museums back to their country of origin.

W. M. Flinders Petrie
(1853-1942)

In 1880, Flinders Petrie began a series of digs in Egypt. Self-educated, Flinders Petrie served as professor of Egyptology at University College, London, from 1892 to 1933. He founded the *Journal of Egyptian Archaeology* in 1911. His many books include *Pyramids and Temples of Gizeh* (1883) and *Ten Years' Digging in Egypt* (1892).

METHODS Many of Flinders Petrie's excavation techniques are still in use today.

Mark Lehner (1950-)

This American Egyptologist, who studied at Yale University, is a professor of Egyptology at the Oriental Institute of the University of Chicago and a Research Associate at the Semitic Museum at Harvard University. Since 1984, he has been director of the Giza Plateau Mapping Project. He worked on the tomb of Khufu and that of Khufu's mother. Thanks to Lehner's work at Giza, remains of what appear to be the homes and workshops of the laborers who built the pyramids were discovered, as well as a huge cemetery with graves of hundreds of people buried beside the pyramids. His book *The Complete Pyramids* (1997) is considered a classic of Egyptology. He found that the workers who built the pyramids were not slaves, but free Egyptians, dedicated to building a memorial to their god-king.

CONTRIBUTIONS TO GIZA

Along with Zahi Hawass, Mark Lehner discovered the town on the plain of Giza, which they identified as the "city of the builders" of the surrounding pyramids.

> *"From all indications, it was not slaves who carried out the task of building the pyramids, but rather workers from different parts of Egypt."*
>
> Mark Lehner

Jean-Philippe Lauer
(1902-2001)

The most famous of French Egyptologists, Lauer dedicated his adult life to the study of the ancient Nile culture, a commitment that began in the heyday of the excavations in Egypt and continued until the 2000's, when he died at age 99. Much of his work was devoted to the restoration of the pyramids of Saqqarah. He restored the limestone walls of the enclosure of Zoser's mortuary complex, built around the famous "step" pyramid.

WORKS Lauer excavated the cemetery complex of Zoser and restored many buildings there. He also reconstructed part of Zoser's Temple of *Ka* (spirit).

The Cities of the Pyramids

Life around the pyramids did not end with the completion of the works and the burial of the *pharaoh* (king). Cities were also built to house the officials who oversaw the work. These officials handled the accounts for the works. Their permanent residences were most likely elsewhere.

Scribes (record keepers), priests, and other people lived in *adobe* (dried clay) buildings built around the pyramids, along with the laborers who were involved in the construction. All this activity was documented on *papyrus* (puh PY ruhs, paperlike writing material) records. In Giza, east of the pyramid of Menkaure, the remains of one of these temporary cities was discovered by chance.

After completion of the pyramid, the Egyptian authorities faced the same problem that all states that promoted the construction of giant works had to solve: maintenance. Towards the end of the Old Kingdom, Egypt had 20 pyramids with their respective temples, constructed with materials that varied in quality and durability. According to scholars, there was no established maintenance policy. Pharaohs decided how much money they were willing to devote to maintenance for the monuments.

At the time of the New Kingdom a general policy was established on replacing the old temples, ruined by the passage of time, with others constructed with more solid materials.

PYRAMID OF MENKAURE
In excavations conducted around this pyramid, traces of a small town adjoining the massive structure were found.

Sculptures of Amazing Quality

Egyptologists found dust-covered sculptures of great historical and artistic value buried in rubble by the pyramid of Menkaure. Examples include this *triad* (group of three) showing the pharaoh accompanied by two other figures. This is considered to be one of the best of the Old Kingdom sculptures. Slabs of *alabaster*, a fine white stone used for sculptures, were also found, as well as some smaller statues which were probably idols of worship for the ancient Egyptians.

TRIAD OF MENKAURE
This statue depicts the Pharaoh Menkaure (center), with the goddess Hathor on one side (left), and a female representation of Upper Egypt on the other side (right).

THE SPHINX OF GIZA

Carved from a large natural limestone ledge, Egyptologists believe the human head may represent pharaoh Khafre, who commissioned the work, with a lion's body. Behind it, to the right, is the pyramid of Khufu, and to its left the Pyramid of Khafre.

was Heinrich Menu von Minutoli (1772-1846), a Prussian general who explored Egypt between 1820 and 1821. British scholar W. M. Flinders Petrie began a series of mapping and excavations in Egypt in 1880 that resulted in important discoveries. He served as professor of Egyptology at University College, London, from 1892 to 1933. In 1894, he founded the British School of Archaeology in Egypt. He also began the *Journal of Egyptian Archaeology* in 1911. Egyptian-born scholar Alexander Badawy (1913-1986) authored im-portant works on ancient Egyptian architecture in the 1900's. French architect Jean-Philippe Lauer was considered the foremost expert in pyramid construction techniques and methods. Lauer worked at Saqqarah from 1926 until 2001.

One of the more important figures in recent Egyptology is American Mark Lehner. He created a computerized reconstruction of the Great Sphinx of Giza and is author of a series of important works on the Great Pyramid. Another important modern scholar, Egyptian Zahi Hawass, is a famed Egyptologist. He has directed many excavations in Giza and Saqqarah, where he made many important discoveries. From 2002 to 2009, he served as Secretary General of the Supreme Council of Antiquities of Egypt. Lehner and Hawass share the modern view that the pyramids are not just memorial tombs. They believe the pyramids were elements of a massive ancient Egyptian architectural complex used to fulfill the important role of binding the entire society around the worship of a pharaoh-god.

The Great Pyramid of Giza

Pharaoh Khufu ordered the building of his pyramid around 2550 B.C. The largest in the world, it is often called the Great Pyramid. For more than 3,800 years, it was the tallest human-made structure in the world. Scholars know little about Khufu's life, in part because his tomb was robbed of its contents by 2150 B.C.

A monumental work

Experts believe some 4,000 builders worked for nearly 30 years on the construction of this pyramid which, when completed, weighed about 6 million tons (5.4 million metric tons).

Location
The pyramid is on the Giza plateau, southwest of Cairo.

Height
The original height of the Great Pyramid, 480 feet (146 meters), was reduced by erosion to 450 feet (137 meters).

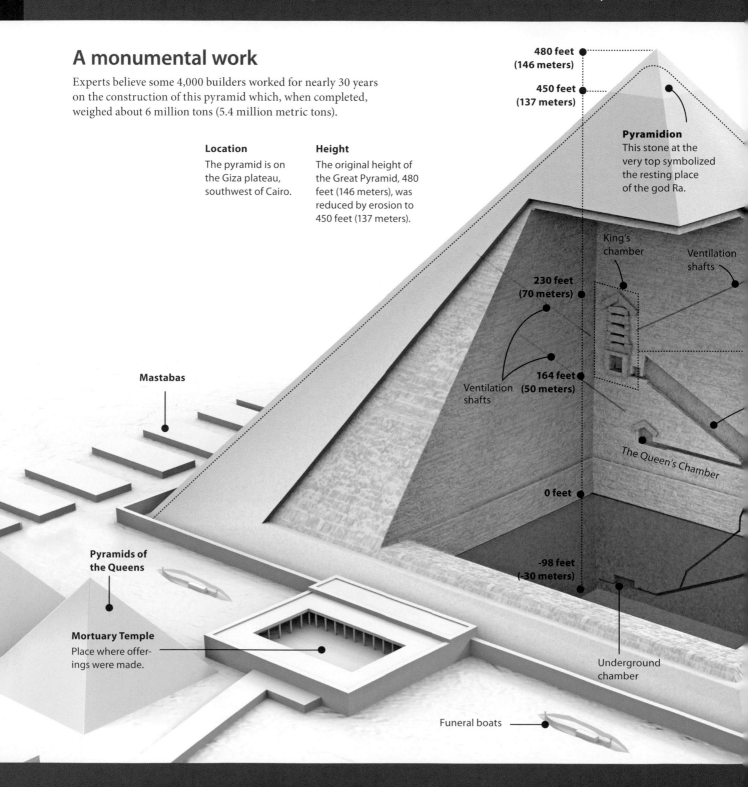

480 feet (146 meters)

450 feet (137 meters)

Pyramidion
This stone at the very top symbolized the resting place of the god Ra.

King's chamber

Ventilation shafts

230 feet (70 meters)

164 feet (50 meters)

Ventilation shafts

The Queen's Chamber

0 feet

-98 feet (-30 meters)

Mastabas

Pyramids of the Queens

Mortuary Temple
Place where offerings were made.

Underground chamber

Funeral boats

How Was the Construction of the Great Pyramid Organized?

According to the analysis of Egyptologist Mark Lehner, the builders would have set up a construction camp in the Giza plain and established a harbor on the shore of the nearby Nile River to receive such essential raw material as limestone blocks cut from quarries. Much about the construction zone is unknown because it was buried by a more recent town close to Giza.

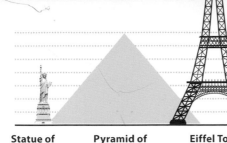

Statue of Liberty
USA, 1886

Pyramid of Khufu
Egypt, 2550 B.C.

Eiffel Tower
France, 1889

Khafre's Pyramid
Egypt, 2520 B.C.

Pyramid of Menkaure
Egypt, 2490 B.C.

The original cover was of fine white limestone, which shone in the sunlight.

The Great Pyramid consists of about 2,500,000 blocks of stone, each with an average weight of 2.5 tons (2.3 metric tons), although there were also some larger blocks.

The King's Chamber

The final resting place of Pharaoh Khufu is made of granite. The roof stones weigh about 55 tons (50 metric tons) each.

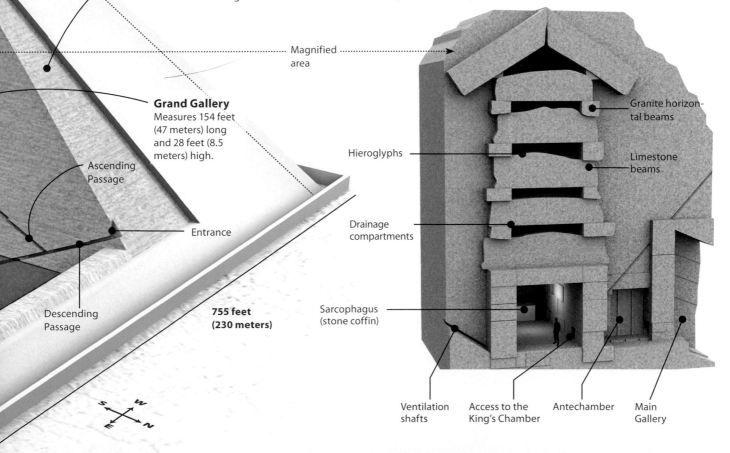

Magnified area

Grand Gallery
Measures 154 feet (47 meters) long and 28 feet (8.5 meters) high.

Ascending Passage

Entrance

Descending Passage

755 feet (230 meters)

Hieroglyphs

Drainage compartments

Sarcophagus (stone coffin)

Granite horizontal beams

Limestone beams

Ventilation shafts

Access to the King's Chamber

Antechamber

Main Gallery

The Pyramid of Zoser

This step pyramid was built during the Old Kingdom of Egypt. Near the main city of Memphis, on the eastern bank of the Nile River, it was the first large pyramid built.

A Different Kind of Building

Prior to the construction of the Pyramid of Zoser, the royal tombs in Saqqarah consisted of underground chambers covered by a square brick building called a *mastaba*. The Pyramid of Zoser was built by placing six enormous mastabas one on top of the other. It is the first monument of ancient Egypt made with carved stone instead of *adobe* (dried clay) brick.

A MILESTONE Zoser's pyramid was built by Imhotep, the greatest architect in ancient Egypt.

How Were the Pyramids Built?

How was it possible to build a pyramid thousands of years ago that remained the tallest stone structure in the world until into the 1300's, with the building of Lincoln Cathedral in England? What techniques did the Egyptians use?

The oldest description of the methods used to build the Great Pyramid of Khufu is given by the Greek historian Herodotus in the second book of his *Histories*, written in about 420 B.C. He wrote "This pyramid was built on a hill in a succession of steps. The upper part of the pyramid was finished first, followed by the lower part." Herodotus's description was considered reliable until the 1800's, when interior chambers were discovered, suggesting more complex construction methods were used.

Today most *Egyptologists* (scholars who study ancient Egypt) agree that the following steps were used in the construction process: leveling; alignment; construction of underground chambers; and construction of ramps.

1. Leveling. British Egyptologist Flinders Petrie performed one of the first scientific studies of the Giza plain. He found that Egyptian pyramid builders had leveled the ground before they began building on it for the Great Pyramid. He determined that they did this by digging a network of shallow trenches into the bedrock, which were filled with water. Then, they dug or

filled around the trenches to meet the water level until they had perfectly leveled the ground. One century later, Egyptologist Mark Lehner, who made detailed maps of Giza, argued that the Egyptians would not have needed to level the entire Giza plain, but they would have ensured a horizontal support base for the pyramid by using a few narrow water trenches dug underneath the planned outside borders of the pyramid.

2. Alignment. The ancient Egyptians used their knowledge of geometry and astronomy to draw the lines and angles of the pyramids and to orient the sides and corners of the structures in alignment with certain stars. To do this, they used such instruments for observing the stars as the *merkhet*—a horizontal bar carved out of bone with a plumb line hung from the end—and the *bay*, made with a palm leaf rib cut into the shape of a "V." These instruments were used in a precise manner to locate the *cardinal points* (north, south, east, and west). They were also used to align the structures with *Ursa Major* (the Big Dipper) and the brightest *circumpolar* (northern) star.

3. Underground Chamber. Once the land was leveled and the alignment of the

How Did They Shape the Stones Used to Build the Pyramids?

There are still things to learn about the technology ancient Egyptians used for working the stones used to construct the pyramids. A materials scientist studies how materials relate to the things they are used to build or make. American materials scientist Michel Barsoum published an article in which he claimed that the stones were not cut or carved but were cast like cement. Barsoum based this on a work by French scientist Joseph Davidovits, who stated that the stones of the pyramids were made up of a kind of concrete in which limestone, clay, lime, and water were mixed together and left to harden in large molds. However, most Egyptologists do not give much credit to this idea. They have a great deal of evidence that the stones were carved from natural blocks of limestone. The evidence includes cut marks on stones that make up the pyramids and copper chisels and saw blades found at the site of the pyramids.

THEORY OF HERODOTUS

The Greek historian concluded that the Egyptians lifted the finished stones from step to step, using short wooden planks.

future pyramid established, the construction of an underground chamber, excavated in rocky subsoil, would begin. In the case of the Great Pyramid, the small underground chamber is reached by a tunnel that led to the north face of the pyramid. The chamber is connected by a near vertical tunnel to a larger room above ground level, called the Grand Gallery. This room could have been used to house a hoist (machine using ropes and pulleys) for lifting stone blocks through the tunnel as the pyramid was being built.

4. Ramps. Although there are no longer remnants of inclined ramps around the Great Pyramid of Giza, most Egyptologists agree that the massive stone blocks would have been moved up such ramps. Remnants of such ramps have been found at other Egyptian construction sites. Most scholars think a smooth, inclined ramp, or possibly several ramps in a zigzag or step configuration, connected rows of stone blocks on each of the four sides of the pyramid. A more recent theory was proposed by French architect Jean-Pierre Houdin in 2007 after tests were done to measure the *density* (compactness) of the Great Pyramid. He detected a less dense structure in the shape of a spiral inside the pyramid. According to Houdin's analysis, the Egyptians used external ramps, but also another internal, spiral-shaped ramp with openings on the corners through which the stone blocks could have been positioned.

QUARRIES AND TOOLS

Architects calculated that 2 million limestone blocks that average 2.5 tons (2.3 metric tons) each were used to build the Great Pyramid of Khufu. These massive blocks were cut in quarries not far from the construction area, although others were transported from more distant quarries on barges down the Nile River. Egyptologists have long debated about the techniques that the ancient Egyptians used to cut and polish these blocks. Most agree that the Egyptians cut the blocks with copper saws, as iron working had not yet been developed. Grains of *quartz*, a common mineral in sand, were moistened with water and poured into the stone cuts. This slowed the wear of the metal saw blades and made use of quartz's abrasive properties to cut the stone more quickly. Other kinds of stone, including hard stones like flint, diorite, and granite, were used as hammers with copper chisels to finish the limestone blocks.

The King's Chamber inside the pyramid was originally finished with a covering of around 27,000 pieces of polished, high-quality white limestone. Soft chunks of limestone were pounded into dust that could be used as mortar for finishing these walls. Some remnants of the walls still remained as late as the 1500's.

THE STONES

The dimensions of the stone blocks are irregular since they get progressively smaller towards the top. The weight of two of these stones is equivalent to that of an African elephant.

THE RAMPS

The Egyptians must have built ramps and slopes for moving the stones. These slopes were made of limestone, gravel, and plaster so that they could easily be taken apart and removed after finishing the monument.

Some researchers believe that spiral shaped interior ramps were also used.

DEVELOPMENT

The side ramps were built higher as the structure was completed. They were removed when the pyramid was finished.

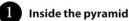

 **1** Inside the pyramid

 **2** Side ramps

The quality of the stone

The pyramids were built with different kinds of stone. Low-quality blocks of limestone were used for the center of the structure, while fine white limestone was reserved for the outer layer. The inside walls were generally made of pink granite and the floors of basalt or alabaster.

Step pyramids

The monument was built in phases. First, an internal pyramid, which had a stepped structure made with lower quality stones, was built using ramps.

Outside the pyramid

In a second phase the external layer was added to the pyramid, using finer stones that left the four sides white and smooth.

Lubrication

While the stone was being dragged, a group of workers *lubricated* (slickened) the path with water so that the skid would slide more easily.

Moving stones

Between 12 and 20 people were needed to pull each stone. The load was placed on wooden skids to make it easier to pull.

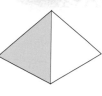

3 Side extensions

4 Finalizing the work

5 Removing the ramps

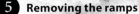

Were the Pyramids Built by Slaves?

Years ago, a tourist's horse stumbled over a piece of a buried wall at Giza. It was a remnant of what would be called "The Cemetery of the Pyramid Builders." This discovery provided crucial information about the monument's human costs.

Most scholars over the past 100 years or more believed the pyramids were built by vast armies of slaves who spent a lifetime toiling under the command of the all-powerful pharaoh. However, recent investigations of an ancient Egyptian cemetery by Mark Lehner and Zahi Hawass refuted this long-held theory. The cemetery was discovered in the ceremonial area of the Giza Plain, south of the pyramids. The experts reasoned if the graves belonged to slaves, they would not have been placed that close to the tombs of pharaohs. The graves of 30 foremen and around 600 workers were found, but other burial grounds exist nearby. These graves confirm that the construction of the pyramids was done by free workers who labored in a large-scale communal project dedicated to the pharaoh in which the entire society was involved.

According to Hawass and Lehner, the number of workers for a pyramid would have been around 10,000. They labored for three or four months before they were replaced by others. There was health care for the sick or injured at the site, and those who died during construction were buried there. Many skeletons show evidence of arthritis in the lower back area and the knees. There were also amputations on some of the workers—likely consequences of the hard and dangerous effort required to lift the large stone blocks into place.

Among the most notable of the graves is one with an outer covering of plastered bricks with several shafts and hollows. It belonged to a man named Idu. The grave's cover had a domed shape, which symbolized the hill where the Egyptians believed the world was created. Experts believe the tomb was built at the same time that the Great Pyramid was built.

Only 5 percent of the total area of this large workers' cemetery has been excavated. Some of the graves had inscribed markers describing the job of the worker buried there. Titles such as *supervisor of builders*, *head of artisans*, or *head of workers' bakery* have been found. This demonstrates a complex and well-organized labor force resided at the construction site of the pyramids.

The Workers' Village

The cemetery discovered to the southeast of the Pyramid of Menkaure was proof that living quarters for those who built the pyramids would have been nearby. Remains of the workers' village (below) have been found, and Egyptologist Mark Lehner continues to excavate the site, which includes homes and three paved streets. The pyramid project permitted the workers to live and be buried close to the monuments they labored on. To the ancient Egyptians, this meant there was a chance that the Pharaoh would intercede on behalf of their *ka* (spirit) and guarantee access to the afterlife.

Well-Fed Workers

On the outskirts of the "Cemetery of the Pyramid Builders" in Giza, remains were found that confirm that the pyramid workers were very well nourished. A large number of bones from fish and cattle, enough to feed thousands of workers for several years, were discovered. This bas-relief (below) from the time depicts a man fishing in the Nile River, showing where the fish came from.

Egyptologists at the Giza excavations calculated that the citizens of Egypt contributed 21 head of cattle and 23 sheep every day to feed the workers who built the pyramids. The meat and fish were generally grilled or dried and preserved in salt. The most valued fish was mullet, a fish that is common in the Nile River where it meets the Mediterranean Sea.

Construction Work

The massive effort required to build the Egyptian pyramids is an unmistakable reflection of the wealth and power held by such pharaohs from the Old Kingdom as Zoser, Snefru, Khufu, and Khafre. They also demonstrate the organizational capacity of Egyptian society to carry out the task.

The workforce

According to the research by engineer Craig B. Smith, author of *How the Great Pyramid Was Built* (2004), with Egyptologists Mark Lehner and Zahi Hawass, some 4,000 stone cutters worked on the Great Pyramid of Khufu, in addition to quarry workers, stone transporters, carpenters, smelters (metal makers), brick makers, and tool sharpeners.

ORGANIZATIONAL CAPACITY

The Egyptians must have had excellent planning and management methods for organizing the often hazardous construction.

The Ramps

Huge ramps, almost the size of the pyramids themselves, were used during the construction process. The ramps were made of *adobe* (dried clay) brick compartments filled with sand.

WEIGHT OF THE BLOCKS ⊪⊪

Each stone block used to build a pyramid weighed about 2.5 tons (2.3 metric tons).

Are the Pyramids Aligned with the Stars?

The ancient Egyptians knew about the North Star, Sirius, and such constellations as Ursa Major (the Big Dipper). Egyptologists believe that they precisely aligned the pyramids of Giza with certain stars.

Herodotus, the great Greek historian, described the ancient Egyptians as the most religious of all people. Every aspect of ancient Egyptian culture had religious elements. The ancient Egyptian religion was based on worship of *cosmic* (of the universe) gods that are embodied in nature. In ancient times, the Egyptians made observing the sky an essential practice. They developed an advanced astronomy which was filled with religious meaning. For example, the 12 hours of the night were associated with 12 visible stars that represented the "12 Guardians of the Sky," who accompanied *pharaohs* (kings) after death in their journey through the sky on the ship of Ra, the sun.

Therefore, it was important that the pyramids be oriented with the stars, which guided the pharaohs on their way through the afterlife. Amateur Egyptologists Robert Bauval and Adrian G. Gilbert claimed in their book *The Orion Mystery* (1994), that the pyramids of Giza represent the three stars that make up the "belt" in the *constellation* (group of stars) Orion. A brilliant constellation that includes two of the brightest stars in the sky, Orion, as we call it, is named for a famed hunter of Greek mythology. It is easily identified by the row of three stars. The ancient Egyptians associated this constellation with Osiris, the god of the underworld who conquered death. The Egyptians believed that if Osiris could triumph over death, so could pharaohs. However, few scientists accept Bauval and Gilbert's theory.

Kate Spence, *Egyptologist* (scientist who studies ancient Egypt) at Cambridge University in the United Kingdom, has proposed a theory that ancient Egyptian builders aligned the Great Pyramid at Giza with two *circumpolar* (northern) stars: Kochab and Mizar. Knowing that the stars have shifted their positions in the sky since ancient times, Spence calculated that these two stars would have been in perfect alignment around 2467 B.C., and this provides an exact date for when the Great Pyramid was built. This theory is supported by the position of other Giza pyramids that were built later. The orientation in these later pyramids seems to correspond with the movement away from true North of the two stars as they changed position in sky in the years that followed.

The Pole Star

Polaris is a bright star in the constellation Ursa Minor, also called the Little Dipper, which appears to be located in the sky almost directly above the North Pole. Because of its position, Polaris appears stationary, while other stars seem to revolve around it as Earth rotates. Polaris is known as the North Star, or the Pole Star. It has served as a guide for navigators through the centuries.

However, Polaris was not always the Pole Star. Earth's rotational axis changes direction as it revolves around the Sun in a process called *precession*. When the Great Pyramid was built, a star called Thuban (in the constellation Draco) was in the position of the Pole Star. Kate Spence calculated that around 2467 B.C., the circumpolar stars Kochab (in Ursa Minor) and Mizar (in Ursa Major) would have appeared in the sky on either side of Thuban, forming a straight line pointing due north.

Kochab, Thuban, and Mizar were always visible in the night sky. The ancient Egyptians associated them with the god Osiris, who conquered death, because they seemed indestructible. Using these stars as a guide, the builders of the Great Pyramid were able to align its north-south axis with incredible precision.

The Constellation of Orion, a Point of Reference for the Egyptians

The three stars of Orion's belt form an angle that differs slightly from the angle along which the three Great Pyramids were built. However, if the movement of the stars that make up Orion's Belt is calculated over the centuries, experts find that around 10,500 B.C., these three stars would have been in perfect alignment with the Milky Way as the three pyramids are with the Nile River. Robert Bauval made these calculations for his book and speculates that the plans for constructing the pyramids of Giza were originated during this time. Bauval believes that other Egyptian pyramids were aligned with certain stars in the sky. However, other experts doubt this idea. They point out that the alignment of the stars in Orion's belt occurred thousands of years before Egyptian civilization developed.

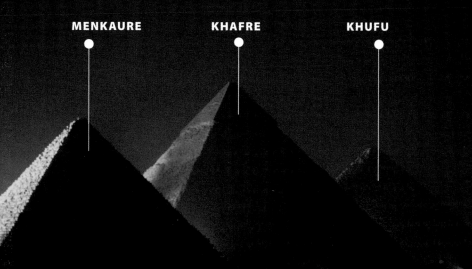

MENKAURE   **KHAFRE**   **KHUFU**

Isis

The Egyptian triangle has sides with a length of 3, 4, and 5 (or its measurements keep these proportions). In Ancient Egypt, it was called the "Isis" triangle after the wife of the god Osiris. It was used to measure right angles in architectural structures, including the pyramids. This simple method allowed the Egyptians to build the enormous pyramids with precise dimensions.

PERFECT ANGLES

Egyptian architects used Isis triangles to form perfect right angles (90 degree angles). Workmen knotted a loop of rope into 12 equal spaces. They stretched the rope around three stakes to form a triangle. They placed the stakes so the triangle had sides of 3, 4, and 5 units. The angle opposite the side of 5 units measured 90°.

SACRED GEOMETRY

The knowledge of geometry, considered sacred, was kept secret by Egyptian priests. The Egyptians learned geometry from the nearby Babylonians.

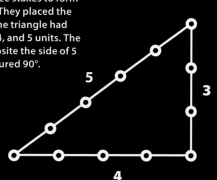

5

3

4

What Was Hidden Inside the Pyramids?

Generally, there were no rooms or passageways inside the pyramids. Underground tombs were excavated in the rock beneath the first level of stones. The pyramids of Meidum and Khufu are the exception.

The structures and passages hidden in the interior of Khufu's pyramid are mysterious even today. Burial chambers are usually found below pyramids. They were reached through a passage that extended down from the north side, so the *ka* (spirit) of the *pharaoh* (king) could exit toward the *circumpolar* (northern) stars associated with Osiris. Yet, the fact remains: no pharaoh's body has ever been found inside a pyramid.

Unusually, inside Khufu's pyramid a corridor leads from the north entrance to several rooms within the pyramid. One of the rooms is called the *Queen's Chamber,* although the queen was not buried there. It was so named by Arabs who explored the chamber because of its *gabled* (triangular) roof, which they identified with female tombs. This room was to be Khufu's burial chamber. But the pharaoh built another chamber, called the *King's Chamber,* higher up inside the huge structure.

In only one other pyramid does the King's Chamber lie within the pyramid rather than below it. The pyramid of Meidum, completed during the time of the Pharaoh Snefru, father of Khufu, is also built in this manner.

COMPLEX STRUCTURE

The structure of Khufu's pyramid has five main elements:
1) The *Subterranean* (underground) Chamber; 2) the Queen's Chamber; 3) the Grand Gallery, an ascending passage nearly 153 feet (47 meters) long and 28 feet (8.5 meters) wide, with smooth walls up to 7 feet (2.3 meters) high, after which the rows of stone begin to move closer toward each other to form a vault (as seen in the photo, right); 4) the Antechamber; and 5) the King's Chamber, in which only a granite *sarcophagus* (stone coffin) was found. This must have been placed there during the construction of the pyramid, since it is much wider than the access passages.

The ceiling in the King's Chamber is made of nine stone slabs. The last of these is *vaulted* (arched), in order to distribute the immense pressure of the stone blocks. There are also several access corridors, as well as the so-called "air shafts," which seem to connect the chambers of the king and queen with the exterior of the structure. However, the real function of these passages remains unknown.

Buildings with Great Symbolic Value

The pyramids were not isolated buildings. They were part of a group of ceremonial buildings that included several elements. What is known as the *valley temple* was built beside a river port used for boats that transported the construction materials. Once the construction work was complete, funeral services were held for the pharaoh, and offerings were placed at the valley temple. A covered passage connected the temple with the *pyramid temple.* Finally, there was the pyramid itself. Full-sized wooden boats were placed near the pyramid to serve as a means of transport for the spirit of the pharaoh. One of these boats was found preserved in 1954, buried at the foot of the Khufu's pyramid. After reconstruction, it has been exhibited since 1982 in the same spot as it was found. Experts believe it was one of four boats that were originally placed at the site in ancient times.

Robot Explorers

The pyramid of Khufu has four narrow shafts whose function remains a mystery. Two of them begin in the King's Chamber and lead to the outside; the other two begin in the Queen's Chamber, and it is not known where they end. Small robots with cameras have been built to explore them.

The Mission's Objective

What is the purpose of the shafts in Khufu's pyramid? Researchers hired by the Egyptian government tried to answer this question, but they only thing they could determine with certainty is how they were built.

The shafts were not made after the pyramid was completed; they were planned before it was built.

The roof and the two walls were cut from the same stone.

The floor was made from a second stone.

The Upuaut Robots

The first robot explorer built was called *Upuaut* (Egyptian for "the opener of the ways"). A short time later an improved version, the Upuaut-2, was completed (at right).

8.3 in (21 cm)

Mouth of the upper shaft

8.3 in (21 cm)

The shafts

The two upper shafts were rediscovered in about the 1600's. The two lower ones were found by Waynman Dixon in 1872.

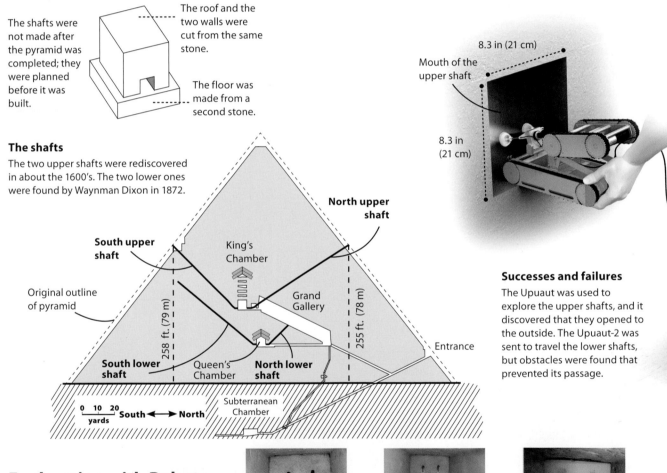

North upper shaft

South upper shaft

King's Chamber

Original outline of pyramid

258 ft. (79 m)

255 ft. (78 m)

Grand Gallery

Entrance

South lower shaft

Queen's Chamber

North lower shaft

0 10 20 yards South ←→ North

Subterranean Chamber

Successes and failures

The Upuaut was used to explore the upper shafts, and it discovered that they opened to the outside. The Upuaut-2 was sent to travel the lower shafts, but obstacles were found that prevented its passage.

Exploration with Robots

In 1993, the Egyptian government decided to install an air conditioning system in Khufu's pyramid. The task was assigned to German engineer Rudolf Gantenbrink, who designed the Upuaut robot, and later the Upuaut-2.

1993
Gantenbrink sent a robot into the south lower shaft and discovered a slab blocking the shaft. It was named Gantenbrink's Door.

2002
A new expedition sent in another robot with a drill and a fiberoptic camera, which showed another slab behind Gantenbrink's Door.

2002
Later, a robot was sent through the north lower shaft and found another door similar to and about the same distance into the shaft as Gantenbrink's.

The Only Objects

Only three objects have been found inside the pyramid of Khufu. British engineer Waynman Dixon found them in 1872, when he discovered the shafts from the Queen's Chamber. They include an anchor-like double hook (left), a granite ball, and a cedar rod, all placed at the entrance to the lower, north-facing shaft. The function of these objects is unknown.

Upuaut-2 Robot

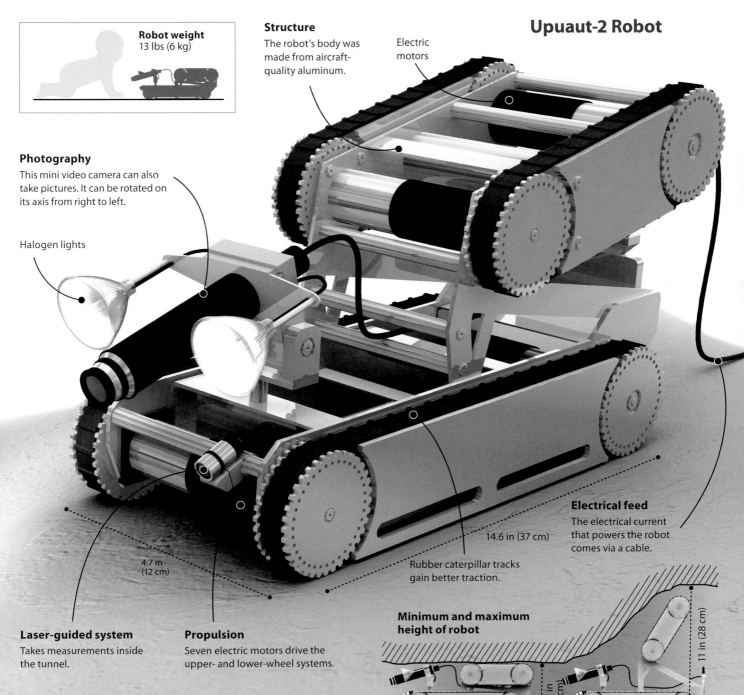

Robot weight
13 lbs (6 kg)

Structure
The robot's body was made from aircraft-quality aluminum.

Electric motors

Photography
This mini video camera can also take pictures. It can be rotated on its axis from right to left.

Halogen lights

Electrical feed
The electrical current that powers the robot comes via a cable.

14.6 in (37 cm)

4.7 in (12 cm)

Rubber caterpillar tracks gain better traction.

Minimum and maximum height of robot

Laser-guided system
Takes measurements inside the tunnel.

Propulsion
Seven electric motors drive the upper- and lower-wheel systems.

4.7 in (12 cm)

11 in (28 cm)

What Do the Pyramid Texts Reveal?

The Pyramid Texts are the most complete collection of ancient Egyptian prayers, magical formulas and spells, and petitions and invocations (appeals to the gods), the ultimate meaning of which is not yet fully known.

In 1881, workers under the direction of French archaeologist Gaston Maspero (1846-1916) at Saqqarah entered the pyramid of the Old Kingdom *pharaoh* (king) Unas, who died sometime around 2450 B.C. Imagine their surprise at finding that the antechamber and burial chamber walls were almost completely covered with long columns of *hieroglyphics* (picture writing) inscribed in blue-green tinted *bas-relief* (carving in which the figures stand out from the background). The room's ceilings had also been decorated with yellow stars on a blue background. Only the west wall of the pharaoh's chamber was empty of *inscriptions* (writings).

These and similar inscriptions found later are known as the *Pyramid Texts*. The writings seen by Maspero in Unas tomb were the first that had been found in a pyramid. They include 228 prayers and other texts that appear to have been written to help the pharaoh in his journey to the afterlife.

COMPLEX INTERPRETATION

The Pyramid Texts are essential for providing an understanding of the history of religion in ancient Egypt, although their translation and interpretation were very difficult. Maspero himself was the first to try translating the inscriptions. But even today, when ancient Egyptian hieroglyphics are well-known and 759 examples of the Pyramid Texts have been translated, disagreements on grammar and interpretation remain.

After Maspero's discovery, more texts were discovered in other Old Kingdom pyramids and tombs. Text passages *engraved* (carved) into the walls of tombs and on *sarcophagi* (stone coffins) of Middle Kingdom pharaohs were discovered. In some New Kingdom tombs, *papyri* (writing materials made from the papyrus plant) texts have been discovered.

Over the history of ancient Egypt, these texts became the basis for what is known as the *Book of the Dead*. This book contained prayers, hymns, spells, and other information to guide the spirit of the dead pharaoh through the afterlife, protect him from evil, and provide for his needs. In ancient Egyptian beliefs, the pharaoh became the god Osiris after death. As Osiris, the pharaoh could overcome death and achieve eternal life. Over time, ancient Egyptian funeral practices became more democratic, and every Egyptian could expect to become Osiris after death as long as the proper rites and prayers from the Book of the Dead were followed.

Types of Writing

In ancient Egypt, *hieroglyphic*, *hieratic* (also called cursive) and *demotic* writing were used. The first dates to 3100 B.C., while hieratic became common about 2700 B.C. Demotic was used from the 800's B.C. In hieroglyphics, some 700 picture symbols represented ideas and sounds. Scholars still do not agree on the correspondence of specific sounds and meanings. Hieratic writing was simpler and was reserved for religious and priestly texts written on papyrus, clay, or wooden tablets. It was replaced by demotic writing, a simplification of hieratic writing, used in such everyday documents as receipts for goods purchased from merchants.

Egyptian Hieroglyphics

The picture-writing system used in ancient Egypt from 3100 B.C. through A.D. 400 could not be read and understood by modern scholars until the 1800's. Once the Rosetta Stone was found, scholars could finally read texts from the time of the pharaohs.

The Rosetta Stone

The stone that unlocked the writing of ancient Egypt is black granite with the same *inscription* (carved words) written in three different forms: hieroglyphic, demotic, and Greek. It was discovered on July 15, 1799, by soldiers of Napoleon's army near the city of Rosetta. It contains a decree from Ptolemy (*TOL uh mee*) V, who ruled from 204 to 180 B.C.

Starting from the Greek inscriptions, scientists were able to begin to decipher the hieroglyphics.

Thomas Young (United Kingdom) was the first to show that the hieroglyphics on the Rosetta Stone corresponded to the sounds of a real name, that of Ptolemy.

Jean-François Champollion (France) confirmed that the hieroglyphics reproduced the sounds of the ancient Egyptian language and established the basis of understanding of the language and culture of ancient Egypt.

Hieroglyphic text (writing of the gods)

Demotic text (writing of the people)

Uncial Greek text (writing of the government)

44.9 in (114 cm)

28.3 in (72 cm)

10.6 in (27 cm)

Enlarged text

Hieroglyphics were not written in linear sequence, one after the other, like the letters of an alphabetic system, but rather were grouped in imaginary squares or rectangles, to look attractive and minimize the possibility of ugly empty spaces.

The Hieroglyphic Writing System

The Egyptian hieroglyphic writing system uses symbols for ideas and sounds. It is made up of:

IDEOGRAMS

Signs that represent objects exclusively in graphic form

⊙ → **r'** → Ra = Day / Sun

PHONOGRAMS

Signs that represent the pronunciation of a letter

→ **i**

These phonograms are what led to the creation of an alphabet.

SYLLABIC

Signs that represent the pronunciation of more than one consonant

→ **nb** → Neb
→ **iwn** → Iun
→ **rnpt** → Renepet

DETERMINATIVES

Signs that act as markers in words to indicate their function

→ Forward
→ Back

The hieroglyphic alphabet

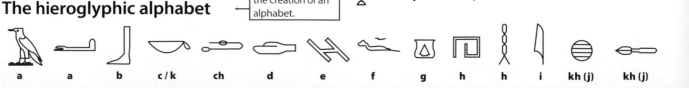

| a | a | b | c / k | ch | d | e | f | g | h | h | i | kh (j) | kh (j) |

The Written Name of Pepi I

Pepi I was a *pharaoh* (king) of the Old Kingdom of ancient Egypt. He ruled from around 2310 B.C. to 2260 B.C. His pyramid is found in South Saqqarah, and some of the famous Pyramid Texts analyzed by many scholars were found in his chamber. This hieroglyph (left), found in Saqqarah, is translated as: "Pepi, son of Ra." For the Egyptians, Ra was the sun god. During the day, Ra flew over Earth in the form of a bird.

READING DIRECTION

The Egyptians wrote both left-to-right and right-to-left. Thomas Young was the first to discover that the reading direction of the hieroglyphics was determined by the orientation of the heads of such figures as animals.

The names of the pharaohs or queens were enclosed in such cartouches (kahr TOOSH ehz) as these.

L **P**

S Y M O T

PTOLEMYS

The heads face the beginning of the words and indicate the reading direction.

The upper has priority over the lower.

With the help of the Rosetta Stone, sounds were assigned to the symbols.

j   l   m   m   n   o   p   q   r   s   s/z   t   u (w)   w   y   y

Places to See and Visit

OTHER PLACES OF INTEREST

THE MUSEUM OF EGYPTIAN ANTIQUITIES
CAIRO, EGYPT

Opened in 1902, the museum is a two-story building located in the center of Cairo and surrounded by a garden decorated with antique sculptures. The ground floor, entirely dedicated to sculpture and paintings, is dominated by colossal statues of the Pharaoh Amenhotep III and Queen Tiye. The funeral furnishings of Pharaoh Tutankhamun are displayed on the first floor. The collections are so extensive they cannot be seen in a single day.

ALEXANDRIA NATIONAL MUSEUM
ALEXANDRIA, EGYPT

This museum holds collections of exotic objects from different eras of ancient Egypt. It is located in a restored Italian-style palace, near the center of the city. It contains approximately 1,800 archaeological objects, which provide a detailed depiction of the history of Alexandria and all of Egypt. The museum was opened in 2003.

BRITISH MUSEUM
LONDON, UNITED KINGDOM

The museum's department of ancient Egypt and Sudan holds an important collection of objects illustrating every aspect of the cultures of the Nile Valley, from the Neolithic Period (about 10,000 B.C.) until the A.D. 1100's. In recent years, the British Museum has worked with scientists and medical experts to better explain ancient Egypt's mummies and how people lived and died in the ancient Nile Valley.

The Pyramids of Giza

The pyramids of Giza stand on the west bank of the Nile River outside Cairo. There are 10 pyramids at Giza, including three of the largest and best preserved of all Egyptian pyramids. They were built for *pharaohs* (kings) from about 2600 to 2500 B.C. The largest was built for Khufu. The second was built for Khafre (to the right in the photo at left), and the third for Menkaure (to the left in the photo). A huge statue of the sphinx, called the Great Sphinx (in the foreground of the photo), was probably built for Khafre.

The ruins of 35 major pyramids, including those at Giza, still stand near the Nile River. Each was built to protect the body of an Egyptian pharaoh or family of a pharaoh. The Egyptians thought that a person's body had to be preserved and protected so that the person's *ka* (spirit) could live forever. The Egyptians *mummified* (embalmed and dried) their dead, hiding their mummified pharaohs in large tombs. From about 2700 to 1700 B.C., the bodies of Egyptian pharaohs and family members were buried inside or beneath a pyramid in a chamber that was filled with treasures of gold and precious objects.

Aswan, the Great Quarry

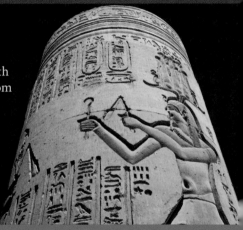

On the banks of the Nile, in the area that today covers Aswan—a city of more than 250,000 located in the south of Egypt—were the stone quarries of ancient Egypt. From here, stone was found to build ancient Egypt's colossal statues, monuments, and pyramids. Under the city, there is a cemetery where the remains of the laborers who built the pyramids 3,000 years ago are found.

IMHOTEP MUSEUM
SAQQARAH, EGYPT

Dedicated to the work of the most famous architect from the time of the pharaohs, this museum is the result of a project directed by French archaeologist Jean-Philippe Lauer. It has an important collection of archaeological remains found in Saqqarah, where the famous stepped pyramid is found. These include the Roman-era *mummy* (preserved body) found in the Pyramid of Teti, and the statues of Amenhotep and his wives, discovered in the pyramid complex of Unas.

FIELD MUSEUM
CHICAGO, UNITED STATES

The Field Museum is one of the few places in the United States where you can explore an ancient Egyptian tomb. The Museum's three-story re-creation features rooms from the 5,000-year-old tomb of Unis-Ankh. From *hieroglyphics* (picture writing), mummies, and a *Book of the Dead*, to a marketplace showing objects from everyday life, this exhibition demonstrates how the elaborate preparations that ancient Egyptians made for the afterlife give clues to their lives on Earth. We also learn what ancient Egyptians might have had in common with people today.

ASHMOLEAN MUSEUM OF ART AND ARCHAEOLOGY
OXFORD, UNITED KINGDOM

A department of Oxford University, the Ashmolean is the world's first university museum, opening in May 1683. The museum preserves a wide selection of ancient Egyptian objects. New galleries displaying these objects opened in 2011.

Glossary

Adobe — A building made of bricks of sun-dried clay.

Alabaster — A smooth, white stone, easily carved.

Bas-relief — Carving or sculpture in which the figures stand out from the background.

Book of the Dead — A collection of ancient Egyptian prayers, hymns, and religious instructions to guide the spirit on its journey to the afterlife.

Cardinal points — Any one of the four main directions of the compass: north, south, east, west.

Circumpolar — Around the North or South Pole.

Constellation — A group of stars, usually having a geometric shape within a definite region of the sky.

Dynasty — A series of rulers who belong to the same family.

Egyptologist — Scientist who studies ancient Egypt.

Engrave — To cut (a picture, design, or map) on wood or stone.

Gable — A triangular canopy over a door, room, or window.

Hieroglyph — A picture, character, or symbol standing for a word, idea, or sound. The ancient Egyptians used hieroglyphs instead of an alphabet.

Horus — The son of the gods Osiris and Isis. Horus is also the name of a number of ancient sky gods. Horus, the son of Isis, was portrayed as a royal child.

Inscription — Letters or symbols carved in such substances as clay or stone.

Ka —A person's spirit or soul in ancient Egyptian religious belief.

Linguist — An expert on languages.

Mastaba — An ancient Egyptian tomb set over a burial chamber burrowed in rock. It was rectangular with a flat top and sides sloping outward to the base.

Mummy — A dead body that has been preserved through natural or artificial means. The most famous and elaborately prepared mummies are from ancient Egypt.

Nut — The goddess of the heavens. Geb was the earth god and the pharaoh of Egypt. Nut represented the heavens. Geb and Nut married, but the sun god Ra opposed the match and ordered their father, Shu, to lift Nut away from Geb into the sky. Shu's action separated the heavens from the earth.

Osiris — An Egyptian fertility god, became the chief god of the underworld. He is generally shown as a bearded human mummy with green or black flesh. In Egyptian royal theology, the pharaoh was a living Horus, who was the son of Osiris. After the pharaoh died, he became Osiris.

Papyrus — (plural *papyri*) Paperlike writing material made from fibers of the papyrus plant.

Pharaoh — The title given to the kings of ancient Egypt.

Quartz — A very hard mineral made up of silica, found in sand and many different types of rocks, such as sandstone.

Ra — The sun god and the most important god in the mythology of ancient Egypt. He was a popular god often merged with other Egyptian deities. Usually, he is shown as a man with the head of a falcon, crowned with the disk of the sun and the uraeus, a cobra symbol.

Sarcophagus — (plural *sarcophagi*) A stone coffin, especially one ornamented with sculptures or bearing inscriptions.

Scribe — Any of various officials of ancient times who wrote and copied texts.

Vault — An arched stone structure built in such a way that the parts support each other, serving as a roof.

For Further Information

Books

Arlon, Penelope. *Ancient Egypt.* New York: Scholastic, 2014. Print.

Dillon, Patrick. *The Story of Buildings: From the Pyramids to the Sydney Opera House and beyond.* Somerville, MA: Candlewick, 2014. Print.

Orr, Tamra. *Ancient Egypt.* Hockessin, DE: Mitchell Lane, 2013. Print.

Putnam, James. *Pyramid.* New York: DK Pub., 2011. Print.

Websites

"Building the Pyramids of Ancient Egypt." *PBS Learning Media.* PBS, 2015. Web. 25 Feb. 2015.

"Egyptian Pyramids." *History.com.* A&E Television Networks, 2015. Web. 11 Feb. 2015.

"Memphis and Its Necropolis – the Pyramid Fields from Giza to Dahshur." *UNESCO World Heritage Centre.* UNESCO, 2015. Web. 25 Feb. 2015.

"Pyramids at Giza." *National Geographic Travel.* National Geographic, 2015. Web. 23 Feb. 2015.

Pyramids: Houses of Eternity. The British Museum, n.d. Web. 22 Feb. 2015.

Index

Acknowledgments

Pictures:

© ACL

© Age Fotostock

© Alamy Images

© Album

© Egyptian National Museum/Bridgeman Art Library

© Corbis/Cordon Press

© Cordon Press

© Getty Images

© Nicholas Reeves

© Shutterstock

© Album/Prisma/SuperStock

© Thinkstock